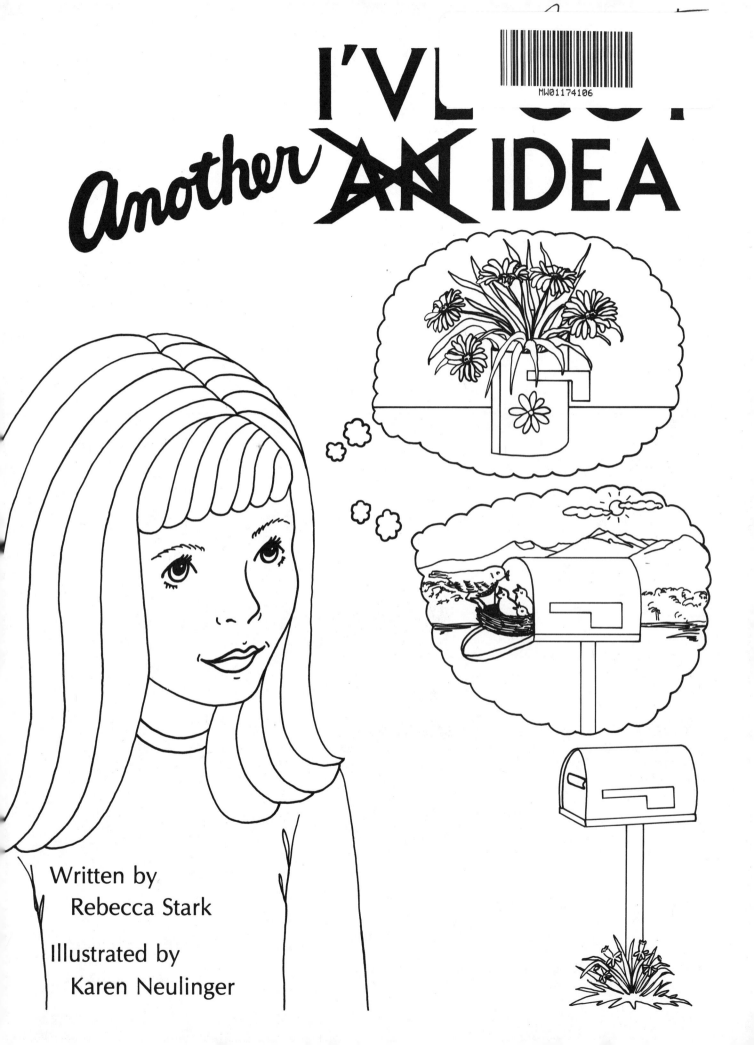

ISBN: 0-910857-55-5

Copyright 1988 Educational Impressions, Inc.

EDUCATIONAL IMPRESSIONS, INC.
Hawthorne, NJ 07507

Table of Contents

TO THE TEACHER 4

WILLIAMS' MODEL 5

Embellish It 6

Waste Not, Want Not 7

I'd Rather Be Me! 8

New in Town 9

An Invitation 10

Pick a Partner 11

And the Sixth One Stayed Home 12

I'm Not Him! 13

From a Bird's Eye View 14

Well, It's Different, Anyway! 15

No Forwarding Address 16

Triangle Art 17

How the Elephant Got Its Trunk 18

For a Change of Pace 19

Say It Again, Fido 20

As Others See Me 21

Strange Transportation 22

Can I Keep It? 23

The Magic Ring 24

A Bathtub Plus 25

If You Were a 26

An Act of Heroism 27

A Sticky Situation 28

Animal-Sitter 29

Excuses, Excuses 30

What's a Typewriter? 31

Feeling Cozy 32

Bend Me 33

A Football Helmet 34

That Tickles 35

Unicorns 36

A Better TV 37

Happy Birthday, Dear. 38

Pets for Sale 39

A Chilly 90° Fahrenheit 40

Buzz Like a Bee 41

My Stepsister, Cinderella 42

What's a Cigarette? 43

A Pool of Jello 44

An Itchy Situation 45

A Lunchbox for _____ 46

Penguins on Strike! 47

That's Absurd! 48

Don't Go, Little Red Riding Hood! 49

Defamation of Character 50

From Sky to Nursery 51

An Overused Verb 52

What Can You Make of These? 53

A Better Desk 54

A Long Way to Go 55

What a Slob! 56

Hamster Haven 57

The First Day of School 58

At Your Service 59

To Tell or Not to Tell 60

You've Won! 61

What's for Dessert? 62

Point of View 63

Signs of Summer 64

TO THE TEACHER

I've Got Another Idea was designed to extend the creativity of your students and to provide them with opportunities to stretch their imaginations. The open-ended activities focus on the cognitive and affective pupil behaviors described in Frank E. Williams' Model: fluent thinking, flexible thinking, original thinking, elaborate thinking, risk-taking, complexity, curiosity, and imagination. A summary of these behaviors is given on the following page.

In order to make creative decisions, children must first speculate on what might be rather than to focus on what is. They must learn to see things from others' viewpoints. They must learn to restate problems in order to recognize the true problems and to produce and consider a variety of alternate solutions to those problems.

Teachers, therefore, are urged to encourage youngsters to defer judgment of their ideas until they have produced many alternatives. They should remind them that there are no ''right'' or ''wrong'' answers so that children will let their imaginations run wild. Praise their most creative, unusual ideas and they, in turn, will be motivated to produce clever, original ideas in addition to the obvious, habitual ones!

Rebecca Stark

A SUMMARY OF WILLIAMS' MODEL

COGNITIVE-INTELLECTIVE

Fluent thinking – to generate a great number of relevant responses.

Flexible thinking – to take different approaches in order to generate different categories of thought.

Original thinking – to think in novel or unique ways in order to produce unusual responses and clever ideas.

Elaborative thinking – to add on to, or embellish upon, an idea.

AFFECTIVE-FEELING

Risk-taking – to have courage to expose yourself to failure or criticism and to defend your ideas.

Complexity – to be challenged to seek alternatives and to delve into intricate problems or ideas.

Curiosity – to be inquisitive and to be willing to follow hunches just to see what will happen.

Imagination – to feel intuitively and to reach beyond sensual or real boundaries.

Embellish It

"Embellish" means to add details. Embellish this rug to make it more beautiful.

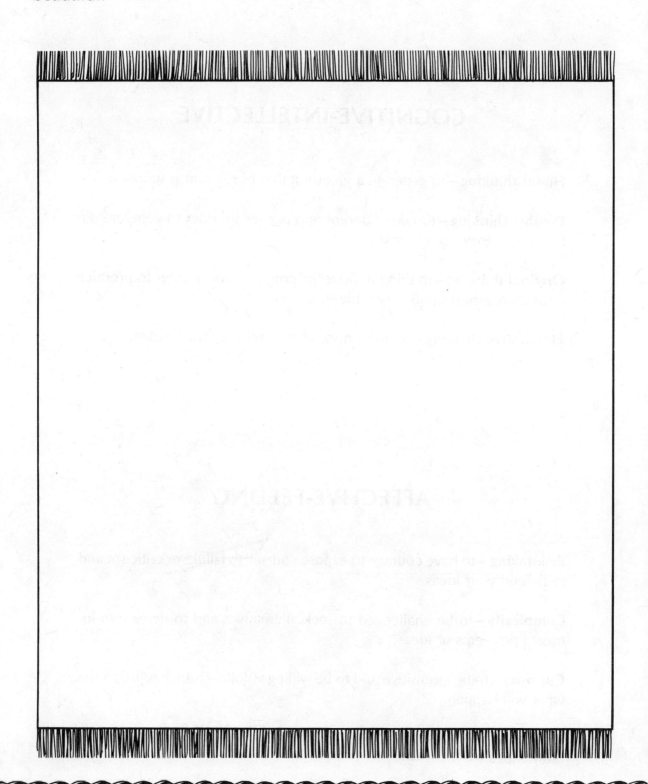

Waste Not, Want Not

"Waste not, want not" is an old proverb. Pretend that you take this old saying literally. Write down all the uses you can think of for your empty milk cartons so that they do not go to waste. Then write down all the uses you can think of for your old shoes that you've outgrown (and no one else wants).

_____
_____
_____
_____
_____
_____
_____

_____
_____
_____
_____
_____
_____

Name_____

I'd Rather Be Me!

How would it feel to be a fly caught in a web? How would it feel to be a tennis ball used in an exciting tennis match? Describe in detail all that you are thinking and all the emotions you feel—first as the fly in the web and then as the tennis ball.

_____

_____

_____

_____

_____

_____

_____

_____

_____

_____

_____

_____

New in Town

Have you always lived in the town you're living in now? Pretend that you just moved to your town from another state or country. Describe your town—its services, the school, the people, and so on. Remember, your description should be from the point of view of someone who comes from a different area entirely!

WELCOME TO OUR CLASS

An Invitation

You have been invited to a party. It should be lots of fun! Most of your friends will be there; however, your best friend was not invited. In fact, she expects you to come to her house as you usually do on Saturday afternoons!

State your problem:_____

_____

_____

_____

_____

How might you handle the situation? List all of your choices. _____

_____

_____

_____

_____

_____

_____

Tell which choice you think you will make. Describe what you think will happen as a result. _____

_____

_____

_____

_____

_____

Name_____

Pick a Partner

You must choose someone to be your partner on a school project. You have narrowed your choice down to two people: your best friend and the smartest student in the class. It's your choice! Whom will you choose?

For each, list the "pros" and "cons."

BEST FRIEND	SMARTEST
Pros:	**Pros:** 
Cons:	**Cons:**

Now tell whom you think you would choose. Explain why. _____

_____

_____

_____

_____

_____

And the Sixth One Stayed Home

You have five good friends. The six of you do everything and go everywhere together! Today, your uncle gave you five tickets to a baseball game. You just heard on the radio that the game is sold out. How will you handle the situation?

State your problem: _____

_____

_____

_____

_____

_____

How might you solve your problem? Stretch your imagination. List all of your possible choices.

_____

_____

_____

_____

_____

_____

What do you think you will do? What do you think will happen as a result of your decision? _____

_____

_____

_____

I'm Not Him!

You are a ten-year-old boy. Your older brother is fourteen and you are getting tired of hearing about how wonderful he is: He's so smart, so good-looking, so athletic, and so on. Besides, everyone expects you to be just as smart, just as good-looking, and just as athletic! You aren't happy.

State your problem: _____

_____

_____

_____

Think about all the things you might do to solve your problem. Write them down here. _____

_____

_____

_____

_____

_____

Now write a paragraph explaining what you will do about the situation.

_____

_____

_____

_____

_____

_____

My Room

Describe your bedroom or your classroom from the point of view of a bird on the windowsill or a fly on the ceiling.

Well, It's Different, Anyway!

Your older sister comes home with a **very** strange-looking hairdo. She thinks it looks wonderful! She asks you what you think! What do you say?

Explain what you would say and why. Do you think you would say something different if she were going someplace special—to a prom or a special party, for example?

_____

_____

_____

_____

_____

_____

_____

_____

_____

_____

_____

_____

No Forwarding Address

You go to your best friend's house to see if he can come out to play. A woman you have never seen before tells you that your best friend has moved to another state. Not only didn't he say good-bye, he never even told you he was moving!

List all the words and phrases you can think of that describe how you feel.

_____   _____   _____

_____   _____   _____

_____   _____   _____

_____   _____   _____

Now try to think of all the possible reasons why your friend didn't tell you he was moving.

_____

_____

_____

_____

_____

Triangle Art

See how many pictures of objects you can make out of these triangles.

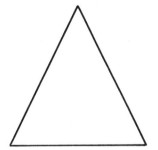 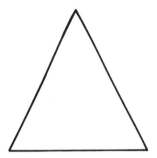 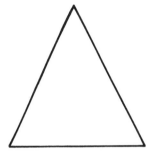

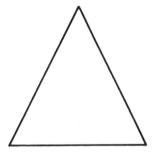 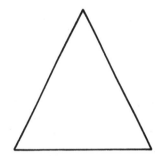 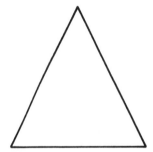

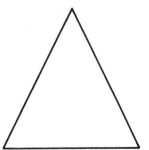 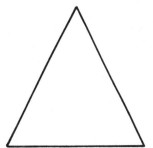 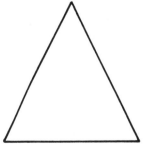

How the Elephant Got Its Trunk

In his *Just So Stories* Rudyard Kipling told a tale of how the Elephant got its trunk. According to the tale, at one time the Elephant had a "bulgy nose, as big as a boot, that he could wriggle from side to side; but he couldn't pick up things with it."

One day, however, an Elephant's Child, who was extremely curious, asked the Crocodile what he eats for dinner. When the Elephant's Child bent down to hear the answer, the Crococile grabbed him by the nose. Following the advice of the Python, the Elephant's Child pulled as hard as he could, and his nose began to stretch. With the Python's help, the Elephant managed to get loose, but not before his nose had stretched into a trunk. At first the other animals thought the trunk was very ugly; however, when the other Elephants saw all the things the Elephant's Child could do with his trunk, they thought it very handy indeed. One by one they went to get their own new noses from the Crocodile!

Stretch your imagination and think of at least five other ways the elephant might have gotten its trunk. List your ideas in the space below.

_____

_____

_____

_____

_____

On another sheet of paper write and illustrate a story using your best idea.

Name_____

For a Change of Pace

Pretend that you are bored with the way your room looks. Your parents will not buy you any new furniture; however, you may rearrange your room any way you wish using what you already have. Draw a picture of your room with your furniture and decorative items rearranged.

Say It Again, Fido

You have just won a dog in a "SAVE THE ANIMALS" contest. When you get your new pet home, you find out that it can talk; however, it only talks to you!

What five questions will you ask it?

1. _____

2. _____

3. _____

4. _____

5. _____

Will you tell your parents? _____ Why or why not? _____

_____

Will you tell your friends? _____ Why or why not? _____

_____

List all the things you might do to convince your parents and/or friends that you are telling the truth and that you are not hearing things!

As Others See Me

Different people often think of us in different ways. For each of the people below, list as least five things he or she would say if asked to describe you.

Your Father

_____

_____

_____

_____

Your Mother

_____

_____

_____

_____

Your Sister or Brother

_____

_____

_____

_____

Your Teacher

_____

_____

_____

_____

Your Grandparent(s)

_____

_____

_____

_____

Your Friend

_____

_____

_____

_____

Strange Transportation

Imagine that you are in class and that your teacher is late. You look out the window and see that your teacher is coming down the street riding on a pony! In the space below list all the reasons you can think of to explain such a strange occurrence. Be creative and try to think of some unusual ideas.

SCHOOL

_____

_____

_____

_____

_____

_____

_____

_____

_____

_____

_____

_____

_____

_____

_____

_____

_____

Can I Keep It?

Your friend's rabbit has just had babies. She offers to give you one of the bunnies at no charge. You want one, but you don't think your parents will let you have it.

List all the things you might say to convince your parents to let you have a bunny.

_____

_____

_____

_____

_____

_____

_____

List all the things your parents might say to you to convince you it's a bad idea to have a bunny.

_____

_____

_____

_____

_____

The Magic Ring

You have found a magic ring. With it you will be granted one wish.

List all the things you might wish for.

_____   _____

_____   _____

_____   _____

_____   _____

_____   _____

Which one wish would you choose?

_____

_____

Write a paragraph describing how your life will change when your wish comes true.

_____

_____

_____

_____

_____

_____

_____

_____

_____

A Bathtub Plus

Think of as many extraordinary uses as you can for a bathtub. Be creative and try to think of some unusual possibilities!

_____

_____

_____

_____

_____

_____

_____

_____

_____

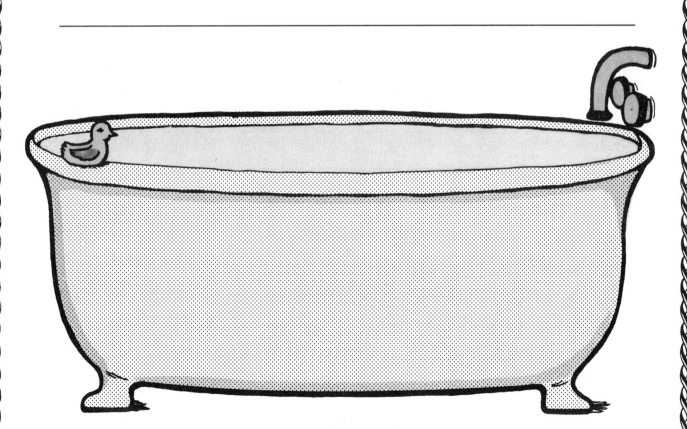

If You Were a . . .

Make believe that you are an animal in the zoo. List at least five things that you would want to ask the people who visit the zoo—first as a lion and then as a seal.

If I were a lion in the zoo, I would want to ask the visitors . . .

1. _____

2. _____

3. _____

4. _____

5. _____

If I were a seal in the zoo, I would want to ask the visitors . . .

1. _____

2. _____

3. _____

4. _____

5. _____

An Act of Heroism

You get up in the morning and look at your local newspaper. On the front page is the picture below. Beneath it is the following caption: **Poodle Named Hero by Mayor**. Also beneath the picture are the instructions to turn to Section 2 to find out more about the story behind the picture. When you look for Section 2, however, you find that it is missing.

List all reasons you can think of to explain the picture and caption. Don't be afraid to stretch your imagination and think of some really wild ideas!

_____

_____

_____

_____

_____

_____

_____

_____

_____

_____

_____

_____

_____

_____

_____

© 1988 Educational Impressions, Inc.

A Sticky Situation

Think of all the things you could do with a piece of bubble gum—chewed or unchewed. Stretch your imagination so that you can think of some really creative ideas!

TRIPLE BUBBLE

Now think of all the things you could do with the wrappers.

Animal-sitter

You have decided to start an animal-sitting service in order to earn extra money. Before you can advertise your service, you have to decide upon a name that will attract customers.

Think of as many names as possible for your new business.

_____   _____

_____   _____

_____   _____

_____   _____

Using the name you like best, create an ad for your local newspaper. Sketch the idea you like best in the box at the right.

Excuses, Excuses

You promised your mother before she left for work that you would clean your room. She is expecting company for dinner and is counting on you to keep your promise. You hear her car pull up in the driveway and remember that you did not clean your room as promised.

What might you say to your mother to explain why you didn't clean your room? List as many reasons as you can. Let your imagination go and try to think of some unusual reasons.

_____

_____

_____

_____

_____

_____

_____

_____

_____

_____

_____

_____

Name_____

What's a Typewriter?

Pretend that you have just met someone who has no idea what a typewriter is. He has never even seen one!

Describe a typewriter in such detail that he will know exactly what it is, what it does, how it works, and what it looks like.

_____

_____

_____

_____

_____

_____

_____

_____

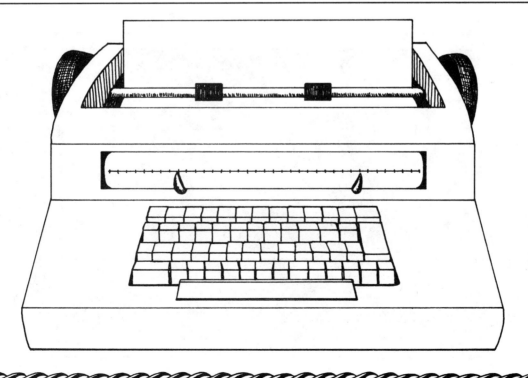

Feeling Cozy

The word "cozy" means snug and comfortable. Many people feel cozy sitting by a fire.

List the things that make you feel cozy.

_____

_____

_____

_____

_____

_____

_____

_____

_____

Bend Me

"Flexible" means easily bent or twisted without breaking. List all of the things you can think of that are flexible. Try to include some out of the ordinary answers!

_____

_____

_____

_____

_____

_____

_____

_____

_____   _____

_____   _____

_____   _____

_____   _____

_____   _____

_____   _____

Name_____

A Football Helmet

You have been given a football helmet, but you do not play football. Think of as many extraordinary uses for a football helmet as you can and list the uses below.

In the box draw a picture of your most creative idea!

Name_____

That Tickles!

Describe in detail what it feels like to be tickled.

_____

_____

_____

_____

_____

Now list all the things you can think of that would tickle. Stretch your imagination and try to think of some unusual answers as well as the ordinary!

_____

_____

_____

_____

_____

_____

_____

_____

_____

_____

Unicorns

A unicorn is an imaginary animal. It is not real. It exists only in our imaginations.

Create your own imaginary animal. Describe it in the space below.

_____

_____

_____

_____

_____

_____

_____

_____

_____

Think of at least six possible names for your animal.

_____   _____

_____   _____

Choose the name you think best suits your animal. Put a circle around that name. On another sheet of paper draw a picture of your animal.

A Better TV

In what ways might you change a TV set to make it better? For example, you could combine it with something else so that it serves an additional purpose; you could make it or a part of it larger or smaller; and so on.

List all of your ideas and tell why each change or modification would make it better.

_____

_____

_____

_____

_____

_____

_____

_____

_____

_____

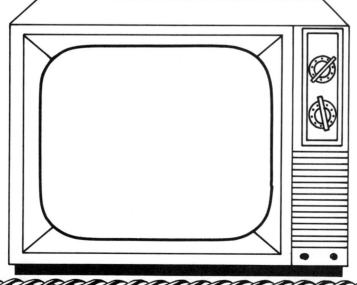

Name_____

Happy Birthday, Dear . . .

In order to earn extra money you have just started your own business creating personalized greeting cards. Choose one of the following and design a birthday card that would be suitable for him or her: your doctor, your dentist, your mail carrier, your teacher, your principal, your librarian, or your school nurse.

For which person will your card be? _____

Create at least five possible greetings or sayings for your card. Then choose the one you like best and design your card in the boxes below.

_____

_____

_____

_____

_____

_____

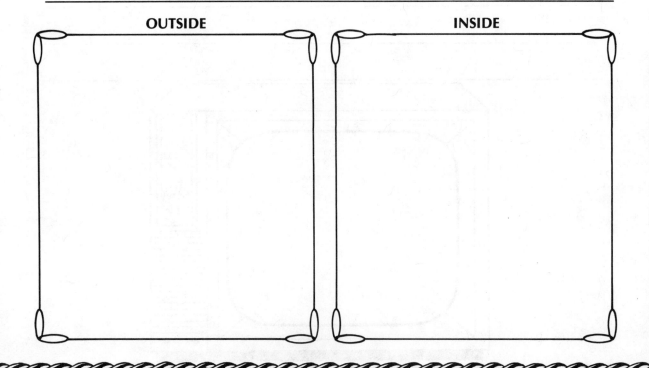

OUTSIDE   **INSIDE**

Pets for Sale

Your parents are about to open up a new pet store. They are having trouble thinking of a name and have asked for your help.

What names might your parents choose that would attract the attention of potential customers? Try to be creative and original!

_____ _____

_____ _____

_____ _____

_____ _____

Choose the name you like best. Create an ad for your local newspaper announcing the "Grand Opening" of the pet store.

A Chilly 90° Fahrenheit

It is a hot summer day at the beach. How might you explain the way the man is dressed? List as many possible reasons as you can. Don't be afraid to let your imagination run wild!

_____

_____

_____

_____

_____

_____

_____

_____

_____

_____

Buzz Like a Bee

A low, humming sound is called a buzz. A bee makes a buzz. Stretch your imagination and try to think of all the things that buzz like a bee!

_____   _____

_____   _____

_____   _____

_____   _____

_____   _____

_____   _____

_____   _____

My Stepsister, Cinderella

Rewrite the story of Cinderella from the point of view of one of her stepsisters.

_____

_____

_____

_____

_____

_____

_____

_____

_____

_____

_____

_____

So, you think that Cinderella's so wonderful. Well, let me tell you my side of the story!

_____

_____

_____

_____

_____

_____

What's a Cigarette?

It is years from now. No one smokes anymore. What uses can you think of for all the ashtrays that remain now that they aren't needed for their original purpose?

_____

_____

_____

_____

_____

_____

_____

_____

_____

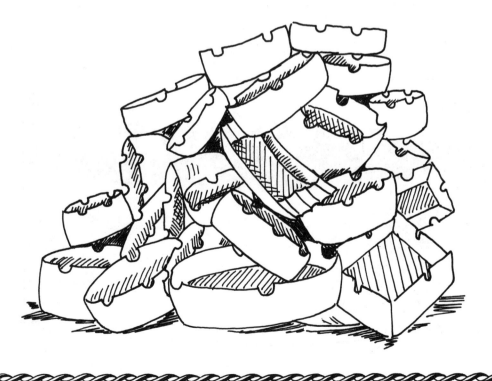

A Pool of Jello

Describe in detail how it would feel to dive into and then swim in a pool filled with jello.

_____

_____

_____

_____

_____

_____

_____

_____

_____

_____

An Itchy Situation

You are at a friend's house for dinner. The main course turns out to be something to which you are very allergic. Your friend's father has gone to a lot of trouble preparing it; however, if you eat it, you're sure to break out in hives! How will you handle this uncomfortable situation?

State your problem: _____

_____

_____

What might you do to solve your problem? List all of your choices.

_____

_____

_____

_____

_____

I hope you like this. It's my specialty!

Tell which choice you will make. Predict what will happen as a result.

_____

_____

_____

_____

_____

A Lunchbox for _____

Decorate the luchbox below so that it would be suitable for a character in a story you have read or heard.

This lunchbox is for _____.

He/She would like it because_____

_____

_____

_____

_____

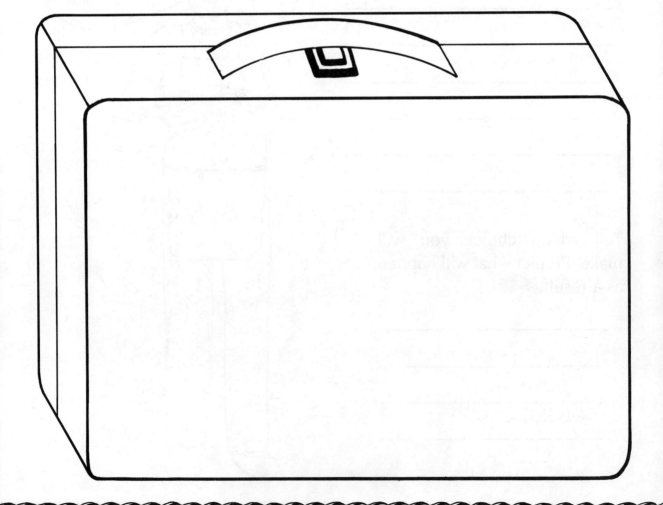

Penguins on Strike!

Look at the picture below. List as many reasons as you can think of to explain why the penguins are on strike.

_____   _____

_____   _____

_____   _____

_____   _____

_____   _____

_____   _____

_____   _____

_____   _____

_____   _____

That's Absurd!

"Absurd" means very silly, or ridiculous. List at least ten things that you would describe as absurd.

_____ _____

_____ _____

_____ _____

_____ _____

_____ _____

From the list above, choose your **most absurd** idea. Illustrate it in the box below.

Don't Go, Little Red Riding Hood!

Imagine that you are in Fairy Tale Land. You meet Little Red Riding Hood. She is just leaving her house to visit her grandmother. What might you say to convince her not to go alone? List all of the things you might say.

_____

_____

_____

_____

_____

_____

_____

_____

_____

_____

_____

_____

_____

_____

_____

49

Defamation of Character

When someone says or writes things that hurt our reputations, we call it defamation of character. As the wolf, write a letter to the editor of a newspaper complaining about the defamation of your character. In particular, you are upset about the bad publicity you are getting from the "Little Red Riding Hood" and "The Three Little Pigs" stories.

Dear Editor:

_____

_____

_____

_____

_____

_____

_____

_____

_____

Sincerely,

From Sky to Nursery

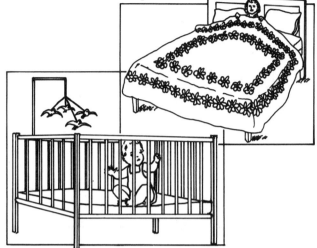

Look out your window or around the room. Apply something you see to something else. For example, you might see a bird circling in the sky; it might give you an idea for a mobile for a baby. You might see a pretty flower and think it would make a nice design for a bedspread.

Try to think of several ideas. List them in the space below.

WHAT I SEE	HOW I CAN APPLY IT
_____	_____
_____	_____
_____	_____
_____	_____
_____	_____
_____	_____

Put a check next to the idea you like best. Draw a picture of your idea in the box below.

An Overused Verb

In our written work and conversations many of us overuse the verb "said." Think of as many verbs as you can that could take the place of "said."

_____

_____

_____

_____

_____

_____

_____

_____

_____

_____

_____

_____

_____

What Can You Make of These?

Sketch objects out of these figures. Try to be original and to come up with some unique ideas!

A Better Desk

Think about the desk you have at school. List at least six ways to improve it.

_____

_____

_____

_____

_____

_____

_____

_____

A Long Way to Go

You and your family are taking a 5-hour car trip. There is little to see along the way. List all the things you might do to amuse yourself. Be creative and try to think of some unusual things so that you don't get bored!

_____   _____

_____   _____

_____   _____

_____   _____

_____   _____

_____   _____

_____   _____

_____   _____

What a Slob!

You share a room with your older brother or sister. He(She) never picks up his(her) clothes. Instead, he(she) drops them on the floor, on his(her) bed, on *your* bed, and so on. If his(her) papers or other garbage miss the trash can, they stay wherever they happen to fall. You, on the other hand, are very neat. You dislike living in a sloppy room, but there is no other bedroom besides your parents' room.

What is your problem? _____

_____

_____

List all the things you might do to solve your problem.

_____

_____

_____

_____

_____

_____

_____

Put a check next to the idea you think has the best chance of solving your problem. Predict what will happen if you carry out that idea.

_____

_____

_____

_____

Hamster Haven

A haven is a place of safety and shelter. What might you add to this hamster's cage to turn it into a haven? Right now, the hamster only has food and water in the cage. Add whatever you can think of to make the hamster's life safer, healthier, and happier.

The First Day of School

Pretend that it is the first day of school. Your younger sister, who is just entering kindergarten, is afraid to go. List all of the things you might say or do to convince her to go.

_____

_____

_____

_____

_____

_____

_____

_____

At Your Service

You want to earn money so that you can buy a new bicycle. List all of the things you could sell and all of the services you could perform to earn the money. Try to think of some out of the ordinary ideas!

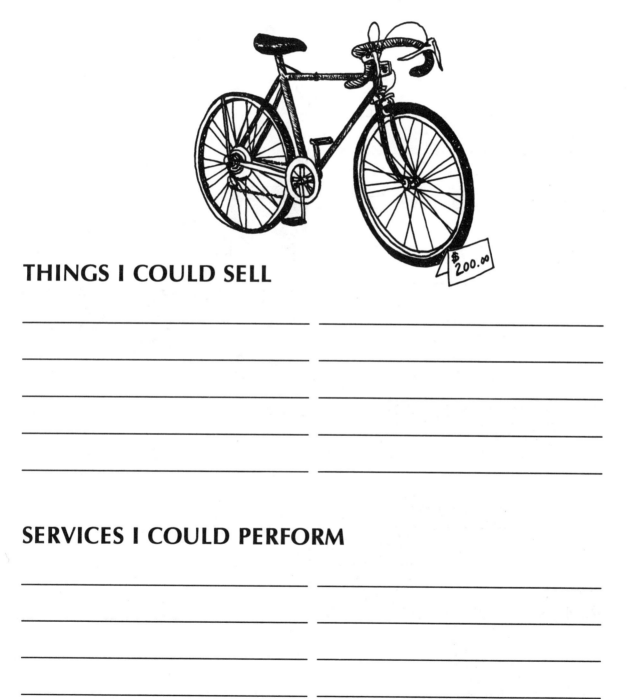

THINGS I COULD SELL

_____   _____
_____   _____
_____   _____
_____   _____
_____   _____

SERVICES I COULD PERFORM

_____   _____
_____   _____
_____   _____
_____   _____
_____   _____

To Tell or Not to Tell

Someone has been stealing things from the other children's desks and coat pockets. You know who it is. The person is your friend. How do you think you will handle the situation?

What is your problem? _____

_____

_____

_____

What choices do you have? ___

_____

_____

_____

_____

What do you think you will do? _____

_____

_____

_____

_____

Predict what will happen if you make this choice. _____

_____

_____

_____

You've Won!

Congratulations! You have just won a contest! The prize is a dinner at your favorite restaurant with your favorite movie or TV star.

Which star will you choose? _____

Why?_____

_____

Which restaurant will you choose? _____

Why?_____

_____

Think of at least five questions you will ask the star. List the questions in the space below.

_____

_____

_____

_____

_____

_____

_____

_____

_____

_____

_____

What's for Dessert?

You are about to enter a cooking contest for the most original dessert idea.
Describe your dessert in the space below.

_____

_____

_____

_____

_____

What might you call your dessert? List as many names as possible.

_____ _____

_____ _____

_____ _____

_____ _____

Choose your favorite name and design the packaging and/or a magazine ad
for your product in the box below.

Point of View

The way we see things and what we think about things depends a great deal on our point of view. Describe a pony: first from the point of view of an elephant and then from the point of view of a kitten.

**A PONY FROM AN
ELEPHANT'S POINT OF VIEW**

**A PONY FROM A
KITTEN'S POINT OF VIEW**

_____   _____

_____   _____

_____   _____

_____   _____

_____   _____

_____   _____

_____   _____

Signs of Summer

List as many things as you can that remind you of summer. Be sure to include sights, sounds, tastes, sensations of touch, smells, and feelings.

_____

_____

_____

_____

_____

_____

_____

_____

_____

_____

_____

_____

_____

_____

_____

_____

_____

_____

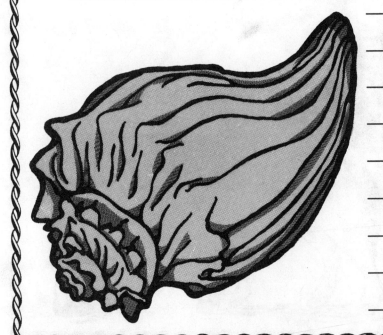